WHY SO MANY
DENOMINATIONS?

THE FOURTH ANGEL'S
PUBLISHING

Printed in the U.S.A.
978-0-9712-0977-0

(817)919-7267
www.fourthangelpublications.com

Contents

INTRODUCTION

The purpose of this little book is to help clarify the question often asked: "Why are there so many different denominations?" Have you ever wondered, if there's one God and one Bible, then why are there so many different churches that dot the hillsides. The world has thousands upon thousands of church congregations and with this multitude of denominations people often wonder: "How can I find the truth? How can I know what truth is?"

Have you ever seen one of those churches hang a sign on its door that says: "Don't come in here, because you'll find error and not truth" or "We have the best mixture of truth and error available today?" Isn't it quite amazing that every one of these churches claims to have the truth? You can start at the beginning of the alphabet and go to Assembly of God and then on to the Baptists, to Congregationalists, to Disciples of Christ, etc.. You can go through the alphabet and there will be a name for a church based on nearly every letter of the alphabet; all the way to Zionists. Every one of these churches claiming to have the truth. With this collection of confusing concepts how can one discover truth? The average person is baffled by this bewildering bunch of churches. They sometimes simply throw up their hands and say: "Because there

is so much error and man-made tradition in religion I'm not going to go to any church."

The devil has many deceptions. One decep-
tion is to grasp on to any church, don't ask any
questions and to be quite naive. The other side
of that coin is to be so cynical and so skeptical
that you rule out everything. The Bible clearly
describes why there are so many different denominations and it helps us find our way through
the maze of confusion. It helps intelligent, thinking, rational people to understand where these
churches came from, and how to sort out truth
from error. As one studies Bible prophecy they
will understand what happened to the early
Christian church, why it happened, and discover
how to find the truth for themselves.

Revelation, the last book of the Bible, was written
for the last generation of men and women to
live on planet Earth. It is the Revelation of Jesus Christ and reveals things shortly to come to
pass. In Revelation we find valuable information
as to why there are so many denominations. In
this book are presented seven churches, which
represent seven periods of church history. Within
these seven periods are revealed the trends and
developments that happened from apostolic
times down to our very day, which lead to the
establishment of the different denominations.

Why So Many Denominations?

THE CHURCH OF EPHESUS
(AD 31-100)

Of the seven churches the first to be mentioned is Ephesus (Revelation 2:1-7), the literal meaning of which is "desirable." This is a very accurate and fitting description of the early church's character and condition, in as much as those early Christians had received the doctrine of Christ in all its purity. As can be seen from verse two, they were highly commended for their works, labor, and patience; as well as their refusal to tolerate or condone wickedness. It is also most evident that the Christian believers of the apostolic church were filled with earnestness and enthusiasm; for the Scriptures reveal that the early Christians were so dedicated to the Lord and His gospel that even in the face of fierce opposition the "Good News" of the gospel had been given to all the inhabited parts of the world by the end of the first century A.D. (Colossians 1:23).

This was truly a desirable church in the eyes of the Lord, but after a while they began to lose their zeal, and their love for God and one another began to grow less, thus allowing coldness to creep into the church, bringing about the reproof and warning found in Revelation 2:4, 5. He also gives them specific counsel as to what they should do in order to correct their pitiful condition. "Remember therefore from whence thou art fallen, and repent, and do the first works." He then warns if they do not repent He will remove their candlestick (or church) from its place (Revelation 1:20).

The Lord highly commended this church for hating the deeds of the Nicolaitans, which He also hated. The Nicolaitans were a gnostic sect that taught that the deeds done in the flesh did not affect the purity of the soul, and that it was good to yield to the lusts and passions of the lower nature. It is indeed sad that by the time the church entered the period of Pergamos these erroneous practices, which both God and His church hated, had become "doctrine" held within the church (vs. 15). As the centuries passed, more and more corruptions began to creep into the church, until today we find a great many pagan practices, which God hates, as doctrinal norms among His professed followers. However, never forget that even though many professed Christians have ceased to hate these things - God has not.

Since this period of time in church history applies to that of apostolic purity it would begin shortly after our Lord's ascension in A.D. 31 and continue until shortly after the death of the last apostle in approximately A.D. 100.

THE CHURCH OF SMYRNA
(AD 100-313)

The next church to be mentioned is the church of Smyrna (Revelation 2:8-11). Since the Ephesus period of church history extended from approximately A.D. 31 until A.D. 100, the beginning of the era symbolized by the church of Smyrna would be approximately A.D. 100.

In addressing this church the Lord immediately refers to Himself as the One "which was dead, and is alive." This is a most fitting description for this was the period in which the church was to undergo the tremendous ordeal of Roman persecution. What comfort the thousands of martyrs must have found in the knowledge that their Lord, who had suffered the same fate, had gained victory over death and had the power to resurrect them at His coming. What comfort we can find in the assurance that "death is a conquered tyrant. He may gather to the grave the precious of earth, and gloat for a season over his apparent triumph. But he is performing a fruitless task, for the key to his dark prison house has been wrenched from his grasp, and is now held in the hands of a mightier than he. He is compelled to deposit his trophies in a region over which another has absolute control; and this one is the unchanging Friend and the pledged Redeemer of His people. Then grieve not for the righteous dead; they are in safekeeping. An enemy takes them away for awhile, but a friend holds the key to the place of their temporary confinement." Uriah Smith, Daniel and the Revelation, pp. 358, 359

To this church Christ gives no reproof or warning, but counsels them to fear nothing and to be faithful unto death. Then to the overcomer He promises a crown of life and deliverance from the second death. Though His followers may lose their lives and sleep the sleep of death for a short period, when their Lord returns they will not suffer the death that lasts forever, but shall receive life eternal.

Although the first official Roman policy against Christians was issued by Trajan, shortly after A.D. 100, the persecution was at a minimum for the Roman officials were not permitted to hunt out Christians. But if a person was brought before them for other offenses and it was discovered that they were Christians, they were to either be made to recant or be executed. This law was never uniformly enforced, but nevertheless remained an active law until Constantine's edict of toleration issued in A.D. 313.

The first systematic persecution of Christians did not occur until A.D. 250 under the emperor Decius. In his decree he ordered the universal suppression of Christianity by means of torture, death, and the confiscation of property. With the death of Decius in A.D. 251 this policy lapsed, but was revived a short time later by the Roman emperor Valerian. Upon Valerian's death the policy again lapsed and the church was virtually unmolested until A.D. 303 during the reign of Diocletian.

During these last ten years of Roman persecution, the emperors Diocletian and Galerius waged the most horrid campaign of annihilation against Christianity to that time. Their decree banning Christianity in the empire was issued in A.D. 303. It is recorded by Theodoret, a historian from that time, that some years after the persecution ended, the bishops were gathered before the Council of Nicaea (A.D. 325) and many came without eyes, some without arms, for they had been pulled out of their sockets, and many others whose bodies had been horribly mutilated in various ways. Ten years later (A.D. 313) Christianity was declared a legal religion by the emperor Constantine. Thus, the period of persecution ended and so did the second period of church history, the church of Smyrna.

Why So Many Denominations?

Satan saw that he could not destroy the Christian church. It was moving ahead in triumph. The gospel was going from city to city, from village to village. So Satan raised up vicious persecution and Christians were thrown to the lions, martyred and burned at the stake. The church was severely persecuted as the Roman armies marched against that early church. These early Christians knew what it meant to stand fast for God.

There are people today that say to me: "Pastor, if I make this decision my husband will really get angry." "My wife may leave me." "My parents will disown me." They say: "if I make this decision, I may lose my job." Or "it's so difficult because I have cravings for alcohol and tobacco." Think about what early Christians faced. Today many desire an easy going, accommodating Christianity. They fail to realize every test we go through makes our faith stronger. Every time we stand for God He gives us the power and strength to do what we could never do. The martyrs did not face the lions alone. They did not face torture and the stake alone. God was with them and gave them extra strength, power and peace.

THE CHURCH OF PERGAMOS
(AD 313-538)

The Smyrna period of church history covers the time from A.D. 100 to A.D. 313. For over two centuries Christianity had existed as an illegal religion, but in A.D. 313 Constantine the Great, the first so-called Christian emperor of Rome, issued his famous Edict of Milan making Christianity a legal religion and granting Christians various privileges. Thus we transcend from Smyrna to Pergamos (Revelation 2:12-17), from the period of persecution to that of popularity. Satan had failed to destroy the church through persecution; now he began to corrupt it from within.

The word Pergamos signifies "height" or "elevation" which is most fitting for it was during this period of Christian history that Christians had to struggle most fiercely against a spirit of worldliness, pride, and an ever growing popularity. It was during this time that paganism began to filter into the ranks of Christianity and the church entered a period of great danger.

In A.D. 323 Constantine professed his own conversion and overnight to become a Christian was the thing to do; not because of conversion, but because it was the religion of the emperor. With them these people brought their pagan practices, which began to blend into the Christian doctrines so thoroughly that it soon became difficult to determine truth from error.

"Little by little, at first in stealth and silence, and then more openly as it increased in strength and gained control of the minds of men, 'the mystery of iniquity' carried forward its deceptive and blasphemous work. Almost imperceptibly the customs of heathenism found their way into the Christian church. The spirit of compromise and conformity was restrained for a time by the fierce persecutions which the church endured under paganism. But as persecution ceased, and Christianity entered the courts and palaces of kings, she laid aside the humble simplicity of Christ and His apostles for the pomp and pride of pagan priests and rulers; and in place of the requirements of God, she substituted human theories and traditions. The nominal conversion of Constantine, in the early part of the fourth century, caused great rejoicing; and the world, cloaked with a form of righteousness, walked into the church. Now the work of corruption rapidly progressed. Paganism, while appearing to be vanquished, became the conqueror. Her spirit controlled the church. Her doctrines, ceremonies, and superstitions were incorporated into the faith and worship of the professed followers of Christ.

"This compromise between paganism and Christianity resulted in the development of 'the man of sin' foretold in prophecy as opposing and exalting himself above God.... To secure worldly gains and honors, the church was led to seek the favor and support of the great men of earth; and having thus rejected Christ, she was induced to yield allegiance to the representative of Satan - the bishop of Rome." E.G. White, The Great Controversy, pp. 49, 50

Because of the many errors and corruptions that began to pervade the church at this time Christ refers to Himself as having a sharp two-edged sword, a symbol of the Word of Truth (Ephesians 6:17, Hebrews 4:12), which is the Christian's only means of combating error and superstition.

The church at Pergamos was located "even where Satan's seat is." The significance of this statement can be found in the fact that when Medo-Persia overthrew the Babylonians, the priests later led a revolt in which they were defeated and had to flee for their very lives. They fled to Pergamos and established their central college there, taking with them the Palladium,

or cubic stone, of their mystery religion. As a
result of this move, Pergamos became the seat
of the satanic system of the Babylonian mystery
religion. This cultic counterfeit had been found-
ed by the rebellious Nimrod when he established the ancient city of Babylon and began
constructing the "tower of Babel" (Genesis
10:9-10; 11:1-9).

The priests of Babylon claimed they built a
bridge between heaven and earth and the
title given to their ruling monarch was "Pontifex
Maximus." Pont = bridge, facto = I make, maximus = greatest; thus, the greatest bridge build-
er. This same title is used today by the head of
this ancient apostate religion, although often
simply shortened to "Pontiff."

As amazing as it may seem this confusing
counterfeit continues today under the guise
of Christianity, for when the king of Pergamos
died he bequeathed his kingdom to Rome and
as such the entire mystery cult was transferred
with it. Through Romanism the title, the keys,
the vestments and the doctrines have all been
absorbed into Christianity.

In addition to Pergamos being the center of the
Babylonian mystery religion it also contained
a temple of Zeus, dedicated to Aesculapius,

the serpent god or god of healing. This serpent god was also known as the "man instructing serpent" who gave man the knowledge of good and evil. A living serpent was always kept in the temple as an object of worship.

Even though there were many among the church of Pergamos that held paganistic views, there were also those who did not and these were commended by Christ for holding fast His name and denying not His faith, "even in those days wherein Antipas, was my faithful martyr, who was slain among you, where Satan dwelleth." There are various ideas as to who "Antipas" is in this passage, but the most probable is that "Antipas was not an individual, but a group of people who opposed the power of the bishops, or church fathers in that day." William Miller, Evidence From Scripture and History of the Second Coming of Christ, p. 135

This could very well be the case since the word "Antipas" is a combination of two words, "Anti," which means opposed and "Papas," which means pope or father; and history has definitely shown us that many suffered martyrdom at that time in Constantinople and Rome, where bishops and popes began to exercise the power which soon brought into subjection the kings of the earth, and trampled on the rights of the Church of Christ.

The Lord strongly rebukes the church for holding false doctrines and tolerating teachings and practices which He had condemned and forbidden. It is indeed lamentable that what had been the deeds of a few Nicolaitans in verse six has now become doctrine in verse fifteen, even though God clearly states His hatred for such things.

The doctrine of Balaam was enticing God's people "to commit trespass against the Lord" (Numbers 31:16). Even so, today, there are those who are more concerned with advancing their own interests above those of God and His people. These will deceive people and allure them into believing they can transgress the law of God, live in sin, and still enter the promised land. Yes, the doctrines of Balaam and the Nicolaitans have become so entrenched in Christianity that without the "sword of the Spirit" (Ephesians 6:17) all will be deceived by the false doctrines that have crept into the church. Every sincere seeker of truth must demand a clear "thus saith the Lord" for the beliefs and practices they hold.

"As the stream of Christianity flowed farther from its fountain, it became more and more corrupt, and as the centuries advanced, superstition advanced with them; and... tales of purgatory, and pious frauds, and the worship of saints, relics, and images, took the place of pure and simple Christianity: till at length, the Book of God being laid aside for legendary tales, and 'the traditions of men,' all these corruptions were collected into a regular system of superstition and oppression."   J.C. Woodhouse, The Apocalypse, p. 146.

Hordes of baptized pagans meant that paganism had diluted the moral energies of organized Christianity to the point of impotence. Church Councils had taken the place of the Bible. Tradition stands in the place of God's word. Human works have become the means of salvation rather than God's grace. Images have been substituted for the ministry of the Holy Spirit. Sunday has been substituted for the Sabbath of God. Pagan practices have come into the church, and the church has become spiritually dead.

The church of today, as was the medieval church, might well be termed baptized paganism. Church councils and church decrees take the place of the word of God. Men and women who stand alone on the word of God are mocked, ridiculed, and persecuted for their faith. The history of the middle ages is the history of men and women that were faithful to

God. It's the history of a church that has fallen, but it is the history of men and women with great courage.

Today the world is in practically the same spiritual situation. Although the Bible is still one of the largest selling books in the world, it is also one of the least read. How can people "come unto the knowledge of the truth" if they refuse to study to learn what truth is. Tradition, superstition, and philosophy are pervading the Christian world today and in their wake there is to be found spiritual famine and confusion.

Dear reader, can you see that unless one understands the progression of the church, from apostolic purity, through persecution, to compromise, they can never understand why we have so many different denominations today. But history clearly reveals what has happened. We are told by Eusebius, the historian and early Church Father, that Constantine in order to recommend the new religion to the heathen, transferred into it the outward ornaments to which they had been accustomed in their own. Images, the worship of the sun, Sunday sacredness, and many other false teachings crept into the church during this period and the Christian faith was compromised. The word of God was substituted for "doctrines of devils" and "cunningly devised fables" and the prophetic words of inspiration were fulfilled that many "shall turn away their ears from the truth, and shall be turned unto fables" (1 Timothy 4:1; 2 Peter 1:16; 2 Timothy 4:3, 4).

THE CHURCH OF THYATIRA
(AD 538-1517)

The "Era of Popularity" of Pergamos lasted more than 200 years and ended in A.D. 538, thus beginning a second period of severe persecution. However, this time the persecution was not at the hand of pagan Rome, but came instead from the established church of Christian Rome. This letter to the church of Thyatira (Revelation 2:18-29) covers the period of persecution of Christians who refused to accept the doctrines of the established church. This church is the middle church of the seven and represents the church during the Middle Ages. It covers that period of time that history so appropriately refers to as the "Dark Ages."

The Thyatira period of church history may well be called the "Age of Adversity," for as any good history book will reveal, the "Dark Ages" proved to be a time of severe difficulty for those whose biblical beliefs differed from the doctrines of the established church. The persecution was so great during the period that the "flame of truth flickered and nearly went out."

The early Roman church began to unite the forms of paganism and Christianity which resulted in misrepresentation of the character of

22

God. In achieving her goals she resorted to practices that were most cruel and abominable. One authority on the history of this period has stated, "In the days of Rome's supremacy there were instruments of torture to compel assent to her doctrines. There was the stake for those who would not concede to her claims. There were massacres on a scale that will never be known until revealed in the judgement. Dignitaries of the church studied...to invent means to cause the greatest possible torture and not end the life of the victim. In many cases the infernal process was repeated to the utmost limit of human endurance, until nature gave up the struggle, and the sufferer hailed death as a sweet release." Ellen G. White, The Great Controversy, p. 569

During the "Dark Ages" millions of martyrs lost their lives while holding fast to the truths of God's Word. It was in the thirteenth century, however, that the most diabolic of all the engines of the established church was introduced—the Inquisition. The church leaders became controlled by an obsession for power and authority, and would stop at nothing to achieve their goal. With their iniquitous decrees and deeds they sought to destroy any who dared to oppose them. Truly this apostate power had become "drunken with the blood of the saints" (Revelation 17:6) and the mangled forms of millions of martyrs cried out to God for vengeance upon her. During this period the church solicited the military might of the state to suppress all whose beliefs were at variance with hers. History reveals that in 1208 the established church proclaimed a crusade against the Waldenses and Albigenses, in which approximately one million people perished. These were the "Dark Ages" in many ways and it is an irrefutable fact that "the noon of the papacy was the midnight of the world." J.A. Wylie, The History of Protestantism, Vol. I, p.16.

Even America was to experience some of the persecution at the hands of this power for in 1565 five ships dropped anchor off the coast of Florida with orders to "exterminate the heretics." The "heretics" being a few colonies of French Huguenots whose beliefs did not correspond with the teaching of the established church of Rome. As a result over 900 French Christians were murdered, making it the bloodiest religious massacre ever perpetrated on American soil.

What man has done in the past in the name of religion is atrocious. But friends, the Lord has informed us through scripture that this persecution will again run rampant in the short time just before He returns (Matthew 24:1-13, 21-22; Revelation 13:15-17). Will you be the afflicted or afflicter, the hated or the hater, the persecuted or persecutor? Which would the Lord have you to be? "Inasmuch as ye have done it unto one of the least of these my brethren, ye have done it unto me" (Matthew 25:40).

In the face of this fierce persecution, God counsels His people to "hold fast" the truth which they have. Nothing can be hidden from the sight of Him whose eyes are "like unto a flame of fire," for the intensity of His gaze pierces through the darkness that has enshrouded His people. He knows the faith and patience of His children and these attributes are clearly manifested to all through their acts of charity, service, and steadfastness to God's word and will.

God reproves this church for tolerating "that woman Jezebel." Historically Jezebel was a pagan princess of Phoenicia and a priestess of Baal who married King Ahab of Israel. She was successful in leading the children of Israel away from God and into a false and idolatrous worship. Because of their acceptance of this false system of religion God pronounced a curse upon Israel. Following three and a half years of famine Elijah led the people back to God and His teachings. Shortly afterwards Jezebel was destroyed by the reformer Jehu (1 Kings 18:1-46; 2 Kings 9:30-37).We find in Revelation where this spiritual Jezebel leads God's people into a false and corrupted form of worship and brings spiritual drought and famine upon the people of God for three and a half prophetic years (Revelation 12:6). Not only were many submitting to this apostasy, but few even attempted to check the course of evil that was developing. During these long centuries of darkness and corruption God gave her ample opportunity to repent, but to no avail. His final appeal came to her in the form of the Reformation, but "she repented not." Instead she launched the "Counter-Reformation" and the minds of many were blinded to the truths of God's word. Remember, apostasy is a very subtle and alluring thing by which any who are not firmly grounded in the word of God can be led astray. Therefore, it is imperative that every Christian make the Bible their only rule of faith and practice.

THE CHURCH OF SARDIS
(AD 1517-1798)

The third chapter of the book of Revelation begins with a letter to the church of Sardis (Revelation 3:1-6). The name Sardis may be defined as "that which remains" and the period of time that it covers is the Post Reformation. In addressing this church the Lord begins by stating, "I know thy works", and then gives to them a message that consists mostly of reproof.

The church of Sardis was not fully what it was intended to be for hypocrisy was found throughout it. They were Christians in name, but their works showed the death of their spiritual life; to the degree that He declares: "thou hast a name that thou livest, and art dead." However, the Lord says there are a few in Sardis who have not defiled themselves and He counsels them to strengthen the truth that remains (for even this truth is about to die) and to take the things which they have received and heard and to hold them fast.

At the time of the Reformation, Protestantism gave the promise of pressing forward to reveal the truths contained in the Word of God and applying these truths to daily life. In time, however, they began to lose their zeal and piety. Thinking the battles had been won, they settled down to organized religion; and as such, God calls on them to repent. History shows us that within a few decades after the beginning of the Reformation, the churches began to experience a period of violent doctrinal controversy. Eventually these differences of opinion were settled by the adoption of definitive creeds that tended to discourage the search for additional truth. This, however, was never the desire of such great men as Martin Luther, John Wesley, John Smyth, John Calvin and other early reformers whose searching of the Scriptures brought to light so many of the truths we hold so dear today. These men did as the Lord commands each of us to do today: "Search the Scriptures" (John 5:39).

As Martin Luther stood before the Diet of Worms on April 18, 1521, he made one simple statement that sums up the feeling of all the early reformers. It is a powerful statement that comes echoing down to us through the corridors of time. "Unless I am convicted of error by the testimony of Scripture or... by manifest reasoning, I stand convicted by the Scriptures to which I have appealed, and my conscience is taken captive by God's Word, I cannot and will not recant anything, for to act against our conscience is neither safe for us, nor open to us." H. Bettenson, Documents of the Christian Church, pp. 282-283

The Church of Sardis   (AD 1517-1798)

All Christians today need to grasp tightly the sacred Scriptures to take their stand solely and firmly upon the Word of God and say as did this great reformer, "Hier stehen ich. Ich kann nicht anderer. Gott hilfe mir. Amen." ("Here I stand. I cannot do otherwise. God help me. Amen.")

Even though the message of Sardis contains mostly reproof, the Lord also acknowledges that there are a few in Sardis that have not defiled their garments. These He declares to be worthy to walk with Him in white raiment, the symbol of His own righteousness, and promises to confess their name before His heavenly Father; the very act which allows their names to be retained in the Book of Life.

Some today declare that once a person is saved and their name is recorded in the book of life they can never be lost or have their name blotted out of that book. If this is true then this warning would never have been given. Even Paul realized that he, himself, could become "a castaway" (1 Corinthians 9:27). It is for this reason that we find such warnings as those found in Hebrews 6:4-8 and 2 Peter 2:20-21. It is only those who continually overcome that will have their names retained in the Book of Life.

THE CHURCH OF PHILADELPHIA
(AD 1798-1844)

The sixth of the seven churches is Philadelphia, the meaning of which is "brotherly love." In introducing Himself to Philadelphia Christ is described as "he that hath the key of David, he that openeth, and no man shutteth; and shutteth, and no man openeth." What is it that He is opening and shutting? The answer to this can only be that it is the door to the heavenly sanctuary. This becomes clear when we consider that Christ is our great High Priest (Hebrews 4:14, 15; 8:1) ministering in the sanctuary above, "the true tabernacle, which the Lord pitched, and not man" (Hebrews 8:2,6; Exodus 25:8-9).

Now, we need to remember the ritual of the earthly sanctuary consisted of two parts: the daily service of ministration for sin, which transpired in the Holy Place; and the yearly service, conducted on the Day of Atonement. This service was considered a day of judgment and was performed in the Most Holy Place (Hebrews 9:6-7). Since we know that the earthly sanctuary served as an "example and shadow of heavenly things" (Hebrews 8:5) it would be logical to conclude that the daily and yearly services of the earthly sanctuary would have their counterpart in the ministry of our High

Priest in the heavenly sanctuary. Christ, as our High Priest, may be thought of as having left the Holy Place of the heavenly sanctuary and entering the Most Holy Place. Therefore, the "shut door" would be the Holy Place of the sanctuary and the "open door" to the Most Holy Place, where He has begun the investigative judgement.

In Daniel 8:14 we have a prophecy that at the end of 2300 days the investigative judgement was to begin and the sanctuary was to be cleansed. Using the principle of prophetic interpretation of one day equals one year (Ezekiel 4:6; Numbers 14:34) this period of time would be 2300 years. In Daniel 9:24-27 we discover that this 2300 year period was to begin with the decree to rebuild Jerusalem, which was given by Artaxerxes in 457 B.C. (Ezra 7:7-14). We are also told that the first 70 weeks, or 490 years (70 times 7) are set aside for the Jews. It is also very significant that Daniel states that from the time of the decree, 457 B.C., to the anointing of the "most Holy," or the "Messiah the Prince" would be 69 weeks or 483 years (69 times 7). Simple mathematics reveal that 483 years beyond 457 B.C. brings one to the year A.D. 27; the exact year of our Lord's baptism. (There is no year 0 between B.C. and A.D.).

Scripture is clear that Jesus was baptized in the fifteenth year of the reign of Tiberius Caesar (Luke 3:1, 21, 22). Roman records were extremely accurate and history reveals that Tiberius' fifteenth year was A.D. 27. It was the fulfillment of this prophecy that Jesus was referring to, when following His baptism, He declared: "The time is fulfilled" (Mark 9, 10, 15).

The prophecy goes on to say that after His anointing the Messiah would confirm the covenant with His people for one week, but in the middle of this week He would be cut off, or killed, and would cause the sacrifice to cease. Jesus fulfilled this prophecy when in A.D. 31 He gave His life on Calvary for the sins of the world. The Lamb of God had come and died; type had met antitype, there was no longer any need for the sacrifice of animals. Christ made the supreme sacrifice for our salvation. Halfway through the last week, or seven years, Jesus died; yet the gospel was to remain with the Jews for another three and a half years. It was not until after the stoning of Stephen (the first Christian martyr) in A.D. 34 that the disciples "scattered abroad" and "went everywhere preaching the Word" (Acts 8:4). Paul, the apostle to the Gentiles, along with Barnabas, shortly thereafter made an awesome pronouncement upon the Jewish nation. "It was necessary that the word of God should first have been spoken to you: but seeing ye put it from you, and judge yourselves unworthy of everlasting life, lo, we turn to the Gentiles" (Acts 13:46).

The gospel had gone to the Gentiles and the Jews had ceased to be God's chosen people. Today no nation holds preeminence above another, but God's people are comprised of people of every nation. "For ye are all the children of God by faith in Christ Jesus. For as many of you as have been baptized into Christ have put on Christ. There is neither Jew nor Greek, there is neither bond or free, there is neither male nor female for ye are all one in Christ Jesus. And if ye be Christ's, then are ye Abraham's seed, and heirs according to the promise" (Galatians 3:26-29).

Paul makes it clear that a true Jew is not one of the flesh, or even one who has been circumcised; but one who has had his heart changed by the power of God. (See Romans 2:28, 29; 9:6-8). However, today, even as in the days of the apostles, there are some who profess to be God's people, "who say they are Jews, and are not, but do lie" for in reality they are "of the synagogue of Satan" (Revelation 3:9).

Why So Many Denominations?

In A.D. 34 (at the end of the 70 weeks, or 490 years) Stephen was stoned, the Jews ceased to be God's chosen people, and the gospel went to the Gentiles in exact fulfillment of prophecy. By subtracting 490 years from the 2300 years, it is seen that there is another 1810 years until the end of this prophecy. Therefore, we must add 1810 years to A.D. 34 which brings us to the year 1844, the year that ends the letter to Philadelphia and begins the investigative judgement.

These great truths, which had been lost sight of during the ages of darkness were at this time rediscovered and set before God's people in preparation for the rise of the seventh and final church and has special significance to those of us living in these eventful days as Jesus is preparing to make the awesome pronouncement: "He that is unjust, let him be unjust still: and he which is filthy, let him be filthy still: and he that is righteous, let him be righteous still: and he that is holy, let him be holy still: And, behold, I come quickly; and my reward is with me" (Revelation 22:11-12).

THE CHURCH OF LAODICEA
(1844-Second Coming)

The last of the seven churches of Revelation is Laodicea, the meaning of which is "an adjudged people." This is a most appropriate name for the last church since the period of time it covers began in 1844 (the end of the 2300 days [years] prophecy and the beginning of the investigative judgement) and reaches to the second coming of our Lord Jesus Christ. Thus, this message applies specifically to the followers of Christ today; to those of us living in this "Age of Judgement."

In introducing Himself to this church, Christ refers to Himself as "the faithful and true witness" and "the beginning of the creation of God" thereby drawing our attention to the fact that He is our Creator. This is most appropriate, for in these days in which we are now living the world is full of atheists and infidels. There is an abundance of those who would mock God and deny His existence. Those who would deny the second coming of Christ, and declare that the world has been progressing beautifully for years and will continue to do so for years to come. It is because of this condition of unbelief that the Lord calls our attention back to Him as our Creator and gives us the warning found in 2 Peter 3:3-6.

"Knowing this first, that there shall come in the last days scoffers, walking after their own lusts, And saying, Where is the promise of his coming? for since the fathers fell asleep, all things continue as they were from the beginning of the creation. For this they willingly are ignorant of, that by the word of God the heavens were of old, and the earth standing out of the water and in the water: Whereby the world that then was, being overflowed with water, perished: But the heavens and the earth, which are now, by the same word are kept in store, reserved unto fire against the day of judgment and perdition of ungodly men" (2 Peter 3:3-6).

We find that the Laodiceans are charged with being a lukewarm people. This expression undoubtedly had a special import upon the people of Laodicea for "one of the chief landmarks of that vicinity was a waterfall over which a stream from the hot springs at Hierapolis plunged. Hot when they flowed forth at Hierapolis, these waters grew cooler on their way across the Lycus Valley to Laodicea, some six miles distant, and were lukewarm upon reaching the vicinity of that city." SDA Bible Commentary, Vol. 7, p. 761   The people of Laodicea were very well acquainted with how repulsive lukewarm water can be and so the Lord uses this to illustrate to them how repulsive their spiritual condition has become. They had lost the religious zeal held by the earlier churches and no longer possess the fervor and devotion required to perform the task of warning the world of Christ's second coming and to proclaim the three angels' messages of Revelation 14:6-10.

The Lord declares that He would prefer the people of Laodicea to be cold rather than lukewarm, but what exactly is denoted by the term "cold?" One commentator has very fittingly described it in the following manner. "In this state there is not indifference, nor is there content; but there is a sense of coldness, unfitness, and discomfort, and a groping and seeking after something better. There is hope for a person in this condition. What a man feels that he lacks and wants, he will earnestly strive to obtain. The most discouraging feature of the lukewarm is that they are conscious of no lack, and feel that they have need of nothing. Hence it is easy to see why our Lord should prefer to behold His church in a state of comfortless coldness, rather than in a state of comfortable, easy, indifferent lukewarmness." Uriah Smith, Daniel and the Revelation, p. 394

Jesus has no praise for this church which has imbibed the proud spirit of the world and placed itself in spiritual jeopardy, but continues His reproof by stating that it is "wretched," because of its lukewarm state; "miserable," because they have not a pure heart; "poor," for they lack the spiritual riches received by submitting their hearts to the Lord Jesus Christ; "blind," that is, spiritually blind, as to their true condition; and "naked," for they have not the robe of Christ's righteousness. It appears that, as with a smallpox vaccination, many within this church have been inoculated with just enough Christianity to make them immune to the real thing.

Although the Lord reproves his church for its undesirable condition we find in verse 19 this rebuke stems from His love for us. Therefore, He continues by counseling us to repent and buy of Him "gold tried in the fire," representing spiritual riches; "white raiment," which is the righteousness of Christ; and to anoint our eyes with "eyesalve," which is the only remedy for the state of spiritual blindness previously mentioned and refers to the spiritual grace which enables us to distinguish between right and wrong, truth and error.

In verse 20 the Lord continues to give a further expression of His love for us by picturing Himself as standing at a door and knocking to obtain entrance. This door may be considered as the door of our hearts which we are to open to Him. Most have seen one of the many pictures of Jesus standing and knocking at the door of someone's house, but the one that carries the greatest of all messages is the one where there is no door knob, or handle. When the artist finished that picture friends told him that he had forgotten the door knob, but he responded: "No, I did not forget it. This door can only be opened from the inside." Remember, a door can be either a means of entrance, or a barrier against it. While the Lord knocks for entrance we need to come to the realization that it is we who must open the door, for He will never force His way in. Not only does Jesus knock, but He also calls to us and says, "if any man hear my voice, and open the door, I will come in to him." Thus, we see that, Jesus has already taken the initiative and calls upon us to respond by opening the door.

We must each come to realize: "Every warning, reproof, and entreaty in the Word of God or through His messengers is a knock at the door of the heart. It is the voice of Jesus asking for entrance. With every knock unheeded, the disposition to open becomes weaker. The impressions of the Holy Spirit if disregarded today, will not be as strong tomorrow. The heart becomes less impressible, and lapses into a perilous unconsciousness of the shortness of life, and of the great eternity beyond. Our condemnation in the judgement will not result from the fact that we have been in error, but from the fact that we have neglected heaven-sent opportunities for learning what is truth." Ellen G. White, The Desire of Ages, pp. 489-490

The closing of the letter to Laodicea ends the letters to the seven churches, all of which pertained to seven different periods of church history, yet each containing a message applicable to us today. This is especially true of the letter to Laodicea, which pertains directly to the period of time in which we are now living—the close of earth's history. It is now, during this time in which Jesus stands at the door, that we should awaken and exert our senses to the fullest, trying to perceive the slightest tapping so that we may immediately throw open the door and cast ourselves upon the bosom of our Friend and Savior, Jesus Christ. Once we fully open our hearts to the truth as it is in Christ Jesus and dedicate ourselves to His service, constantly surrendering ourselves to His revealed will, we will become overcomers and can claim His promise to sit with Him in His throne and share in His power and glory.

IDENTIFYING GOD'S CHURCH TODAY

As we have seen, as far back as the early apostolic church false teachings began to creep into the church. Man-made traditions began to take the place of the word of God. Penances, indulgences, images, a counterfeit Sabbath and numerous false teachings (at least 65) have replaced the truth of Scripture. Church hierarchal systems and human dogmas have supplanted the word and Spirit of God.

During the Dark Ages, the Bible was placed by the medieval Church on the list of forbidden books. Under penalty of law no one could read the Bible and to defy the law meant certain death. But would God's truth be trodden down, trampled under foot, and forever forgotten? Would God allow the church to go from apostolic purity to persecution, compromise, and spiritual death and do nothing? Was God's voice to be muted? Would there be error on the throne forever? NEVER! God raised up faithful men and women who were willing to risk everything to keep the word of God alive. People like the Waldenses, the Albigenses the Huguenots, Wycliff, Huss, Jerome, Luther, Calvin,

Why So Many Denominations?

Zwingle, Tyndale, Wesley, and a host of others. But when these great Reformers died, those who had accepted the truths they preached became self-satisfied and drew up doctrinal creeds, ceasing to search for further truth. Thus different denominations arose. These men, whom God raised up, were used mightily of God; but they had not rediscovered all the truth that had been lost, and their followers only went as far as they had gone. Then in the mid 1830s God raised up a man by the name of William Miller to restore more of the precious truths that had been lost sight of. At this time most Christians believed that there would be either a millennial reign of peace on earth before Jesus came or his coming was not literal at all, but merely a spiritual coming into the life of the believer at conversion. When William Miller began studying the prophesies of the Bible he saw that Jesus was coming literally, visibly, and audibly in the clouds of heaven. He also discovered that when Christ comes the righteous dead will be resurrected and the righteous living will be caught up in the sky. Different people began to preach these truths in different places at the same time. William Miller in the United States. Manuel de Lacunza, a priest in south America. Johann Bengel in Germany. Edward Irving in Great Britain. All over Europe, South America, and Inter America, God was now putting all the pieces of the puzzle together. God was going to raise up a divine movement of destiny that stood on the shoulders of these great reformers. Thousands upon thousands accepted Jesus and the teachings of the Bible. God was bringing together people from all faiths and creeds. Because God wanted to restore truth in his final, last day movement before the second coming of Jesus Christ.

Although there were individuals like Andreas Fisher in Slovakia, John James in England, Oswald Glate in central Europe, and many others that understood the Bible Sabbath; Jesus said just before his coming all truths must be restored, including the Bible Sabbath. Therefore, God would raise up the advent movement that would restore the truth about the Sabbath, the truth about death being a sleep, the truth about healthful living. God would have a movement on earth that believed in the Bible and the Bible only as the rule of faith and practice. A movement on earth just before the second coming of Christ, that believed in the power of God's grace. A movement that believed in obedience to God above man. A movement that believed the reformation truth of justification by faith. A movement that accepted the truth held by the Baptists concerning baptism by immersion. That embraced the truth rediscovered by the Methodists concerning holiness of living. That believed the rediscovered truths of the Great Advent Awakening of the 1800s . A movement that would stand unflinching and faithful in upholding the Bible truths concerning Christ's coming, the Sabbath, death, health, the judgment, the sanctuary, the atonement, baptism, standards, creation, the millennium, prophecy, the mark of the beast, the law of God, salvation, the power of the Holy Spirit, righteousness by faith, and many others that had been lost sight of among the abundance of superstition and error.

As it took the church centuries to go from the apostolic purity to the compromise and spiritual death of the middle ages, so it would take centuries for God to restore all the truths for this final, last generation. Today God points us to the great issues of life and says: "In vain they do worship me, teaching for doctrines the commandments of men" (Matthew 15:9). God is calling us from error and falsehood. He is calling us to gather all the truths together and to be part of his last day people. The Bible says that there will be a repair, a restoration will take place among His people. He says we are to be called "the repairer of the breach, the restorer of paths to dwell in." He says that this will happen "If you turn away your foot from the Sabbath" (Isaiah 58:12, 13). God's last day people would repair

the break in the wall of truth. They will cease
to trample God's holy day under foot and
"Remember the Sabbath day to keep it holy"
(Exodus 20:8). These last day people are out-
lined in the book of Revelation. If you want to
know how to find God's remnant people, His
true last day church, among all the churches
of the world simply let the word of God identify them for you. "Here is the patience of the
saints, here are they that keep the commandments of God, and the faith of Jesus" (Revelation 14:12). God has a last–day people who
believe in Bible and the Bible only. Who believe that salvation is only through Christ. Who
believe in obedience to God. They practice
baptism by immersion. They believe in holiness
of living. They look forward to the second coming of Christ as a literal, visible, audible, glorious
event. They are not just another denomination,
but a world–wide movement giving a trumpet
call to restore all the truths of the Bible. A call
that goes to "every nation, and kindred, and
tongue, and people" (Revelation 14:6).

Dear reader, if you have not done so I call upon
you to get ready to meet Jesus. Let nothing
come between you and God. Make a full sur-
render to Him and His will for your life. It is no
accident you have received this little booklet.
The issues are great. The issues are between

Why So Many Denominations?

God's truth and Satan's counterfeit. God has raised up a last day Sabbath keeping, Bible believing movement to gather all the truths of the past and to lead men and women back to the Bible. Look deep within your heart. Do you sense the tugging influence of the Holy Spirit. Do you understand that the reason there are so many different denominations is because so many people became satisfied with creeds and traditions rather than searching and accepting God's word. They simply went no further than their religious leaders. Don't you want to be a part of His great, last day movement; one who "keeps the commandments of God, and the faith of Jesus?"

Jesus said: "My sheep hear My voice, and I know them, and they follow Me: And I give unto them eternal life; and they shall never perish." John 10:27, 28. Won't you respond to His call?

"Fear not, little flock: for it is your Father's good pleasure to give you the kingdom." Luke 12:32. He calls His people out of Babylon into His "little flock," into His remnant church—His one fold. John 10:16.

Identifying God's Church Today

There are several points in Scripture which enable one to identify God's true, remnant, church in these last days.

1. It will be identical in its life, teachings, philosophy, and theology with the early church inasmuch as a "remnant" does not differ from the first piece of cloth on a bolt (Revelation 12:13, 14, 17).

2. It is to have the faith of Jesus (Revelation 14:12).

3. They have the testimony of Jesus, which is the spirit of prophecy (Revelation 12:17; 19:10).

4. It was to arise after the 1260 years of persecution or after 1798 when the beast received its wound (Revelation 12:14).

5. It would arise after the 2300 day/year prophecy in 1844 (Daniel 8:14).

6. They were to experience a great disappointment (Revelation 10:7–11).

7. It is to be a world-wide movement that will go to "every nation, kindred, tongue, and people" (Revelation 14:6).

8. They will proclaim the "everlasting gospel" (Revelation 14:6).

9. They are to warn that the judgement is taking place (Revelation 14:7).

10. They will call the attention of the world to God as the Creator (Revelation 14:7).

11. It is not an offspring of Babylon. It has no connection with the "Mother church" and rejects her claim to power and authority (Revelation 12:1–17; 17:1–6).

12. They declare the fall of Babylon (Revelation 14:8).

13. They will identify and oppose the antichrist (Revelation 13).

14. They warn of the mark of the beast (Revelation 14:9–11).

15. They call God's people out of Babylon (Revelation 18:4).

16. This movement declares and helps people prepare to receive the seal of God (Revelation 7:1–3).

17. They reject all false teachings (Deuteronomy 4:2; 12:32; Revelation 22:18, 19).

18. They base all of their beliefs upon the Bible and the Bible alone (John 14:23, 24; Revelation 22:18, 19).

19. They will keep all of the commandments of God, including the fourth or the seventh-day Sabbath (Revelation 12:17; 14:12).

20. They proclaim the three angel's messages of righteousness by faith (Revelation 14:6–11).

Candid, unbiased investigation reveals there is but one church that meets all 20 of these Bible specifications. That church is the worldwide Seventh-day Adventist Church whose 18,000,000 members take very seriously the divine injunction to carry the everlasting gospel "to every nation, and kindred, and tongue, and people" (Revelation 14:6). Please accept this as your cordial invitation to attend any of the more than 108,000 locations and see for yourself who these people are and what they believe.

Why So Many Denominations?

Seventh-day Adventists Believe...

1. In a personal, loving, all powerful God. Psalm 14:1; Genesis 1:1; Isaiah 45:18; Psalm 90:2; 1 Kings 8:30; Psalm 19:1; Isaiah 46:9–10; 1 John 4:8; John 3:16; Romans 5:8; Jeremiah 31:3; Romans 8:38–39; Isaiah 45:22; John 17:3; 1 John 3:1.

2. In Jesus Christ, as the divine, eternal, Son of God and our personal Savior. John 17:3–5; Acts 4:12; Matthew 1:18–23; Matthew 3:16–17; John 10:30; Hebrews 1:8–10; John 1:1–3,14; Colossians 1:16–17; Philippians 2:5–8; John 3:16; Hebrews 7:25; 1 John 5:11–13.

3. In the Holy Spirit as Christ's representative on earth which leads sinners to repentance and obedience. John 16:7–15; John 15:26; John 14:26; Romans 8:1–17; Acts 5:32; Ephesians 4:30; Galatians 5:16.

4. In regeneration and the new birth through acceptance of the gospel. Philippians 4:13; Galatians 2:20; Romans 6:1–6; 2 Corinthians. 5:15, 17; John 3:1–8; Romans 8:1, 9, 14; Ephesians 4:22–24; Philippians 2:13.

5. That righteousness and salvation are free gifts of God received by faith, not works. Romans 6:23; Ezekiel 18:4; Romans 3:23; Romans

5:12; Jeremiah 13:23; 2 Peter 3:9; John 3:16; Romans 5:8–9; Ephesians 2:8–9; Romans 4:3–5, 20–25.

6. That the Bible is the inspired word of God and only rule of faith and practice for the Christian. 1 Peter 3:21; 2 Timothy 3:16–17; Isaiah 8:20; John 5:39; Isaiah 28:10; Acts 17:11; Psalm 119:11; John 17:17.

7. That the second coming of Jesus will be literal, personal, and visible to all. John 14:1–3; Acts 1:9–11; Matthew 24:23–31; Luke 9:26; 1 Thessalonians 4:16–17; Revelation 6:14–17; Revelation 16:17–21; Revelation 1:7.

8. That the coming of Jesus, as the prophesied signs reveal, is very near at hand. Matthew 24:3–7, 11–14; 2 Timothy 3:1–5; 2 Peter 3:3–6; Matt 24:21–22, 29; Revelation 6:12–14; Matthew 24:30-33, 36, 42, 44.

9. That Satan is a fallen angel, leading a rebellion against God, and will eventually be destroyed. Luke 10:18; Ezekiel 28:12–16; Isaiah 14:12–14; Revelation 12:7–9; Genesis 3:1–6; 1 Peter 5:8; Revelation 12:12; Ezekiel 28:17–19.

10. That the wicked will not burn eternally, but shall be destroyed. Psalm 37:20; Matthew 10:28; Malachi 4:1-3; Revelation 20:14; Reve-

lation 21:8; 2 Peter 3:10–13; Revelation 21:1–5.

11. That man, by nature, is mortal; and that immortality is received only at the second coming of Jesus. Job 4:17; 1 Timothy 6:15–16; 1 Corinthians 15:51–55; John 5:28–29; 1 Thessalonians 4:15–18.

12. The condition of man in death is one of unconsciousness. Genesis 2:7; Ecclesiastes 3:20; Job 27:3; Psalm 104:29; Job 14:10, 12, 21; Ecclesiastes 9:5–6, 10; Psalm 146:1–4; Psalm 115:17; John 11:11–44; 1 Corinthians. 15:16–23; 1 Thessalonians 4:13–18.

13. That there will be a resurrection of the dead, both of the just and the unjust. John 5:28–29; Revelation 20:5–6; Job 19:25–27; Psalm 17:15; 1 Corinthians15:16–23, 51–55; 1 Thessalonians 4:13–18.

14. That the 1000 years, known as the millennium, begins at the coming of Jesus; at which time Satan will be confined to this desolate earth. Revelation 20:1–6; John 5:28–29; 1 Corinthians. 6:2–3; Jeremiah 4:23–27; Jeremiah 25:30–33; Revelation 20:7; Revelation 21:2; Revelation 20:8–9; Psalm 37:20; Malachi 4:1–3; Revelation 20:14; 2 Peter 3:10–13; Isaiah 65:21–25; Revelation 21:3–5.

15. That the law of ten commandments are eternal and to transgress the law has always constituted sin. 1 John 3:4; Romans 4:15; Ezekiel 28:14–15; Genesis 4:7–11; Genesis 13:13; Genesis 26:5; Genesis 36:9; Exodus 16:4, 23–28; Matthew 5:17–19; Romans 3:31; Revelation 14:12; Revelation 22:14; Psalm 111:7–8; John 14:15, 21, 23.

16. That the ceremonial law, of ordinances and sacrifices, ended when they met their fulfillment in the death of Jesus. Deuteronomy 31:24–26; Hebrews 9:6–12; Ephesians 2:15; Colossians 2:14–17; Daniel 9:27; Matthew 27:50–51.

17. That the earth was created in six literal days. Genesis 1:1, 2, 26; Hebrews 1:2; John 1:1–3, 14; Psalm 33:6–9; Isaiah 45:18; Exodus 20:11; Colossians 1:16–17; 2 Peter 3:3-5; Revelation 14:7.

18. That the seventh day of the week is the Sabbath of the Lord and is to be observed from sunset Friday to sunset Saturday. Revelation 1:10; Mark 2:28; Genesis 2:1–3; Luke 13:52–56; Luke 24:1; Mark 2:27; Exodus 16:23–28; Exodus 20:8–11; Luke 4:16; Matthew 24:20; Acts 13:42, 44; 16:13; 17:2; 18:4; Isaiah 66:22–23; Leviticus 23:32; Ezekiel 20:12, 20; Hebrews 4:3–4, 8–11; Isaiah 58:12–13.

19. That at the end of the 2300 day/year prophecy Jesus began the final phase of His ministry preparatory to His coming; that of the investigative judgment, the cleansing of the sanctuary. Daniel 8:14; Daniel 9:25; Exodus 25:8–9; Hebrews 8:1–2, 5; Exodus 26:33; Hebrews 9:6–7; Leviticus 16:7–9, 15–16, 20–22; Leviticus 23:26–29; Hebrews 4:14–16; Hebrews 7:24–27; Hebrews 9:11–12; Revelation 14:6–7; Revelation 22:11–12.

20. In the support of the gospel through tithes and offerings. Psalm 50:10–12; Haggai 2:8; 1 Corinthians. 6:19–20; Genesis 1:21; Leviticus 27:30–32; Numbers 18:21; 1 Corinthians. 9:13–14; Proverbs 3:9; Matthew 23:23; Malachi 3:8–12; 2 Corinthians. 9:6–7.

21. That baptism by immersion is the only biblical baptism. Ephesians 4:5; John 3:5; Matthew 3:13–17; John 3:23; Acts 8:38; Matthew 28:19–20; Mark 16:15–16; Acts 2:37–38, 41; Romans 6:3–6; Galatians 3:27–29; 2 Corinthians. 6:2; Acts 22:16.

22. In the ordinances of foot washing and the Lord's supper. John 13:4–17; Matthew 26:26–29; 1 Corinthians.11:23–30.

23. That the Seventh-day Adventist church is

the remnant church of Bible prophecy, into which people of every nation, race, class, and language are invited and accepted. Revelation 12:1–2; Jeremiah 6:2; Isaiah 51:16; Revelation 17:1–6; Revelation 18:1–5; John 10:16; Revelation 14:1–12; Revelation 12:3–9, 13–14, 17; Revelation 19:10; John 10:27–28.

24. That the church is to come behind in none of the gifts of the Spirit, including the spirit of prophecy. 1 Corinthians. 1:5–7; Ephesians 4:8–14; Amos 3:7; Revelation 12:17; Revelation 19:10; 1 Thessalonians 5:20–21; 2 Chronicles 20:20.

25. That the Christian is to recognize his/her body as the temple of the Holy Spirit and to abstain from that which is harmful or forbidden. 1 Corinthians. 3:16–17; 6:19–20; 1 Corinthians.10:31; Leviticus 11:1–8; Proverbs 23:29–32; Isaiah 66:15–17.

26. That the Christian is to shun worldly practices and maxims. Proverbs 16:25; 2 Corinthians. 6:15–18; Exodus 33:5-6; Judges 8:24; Genesis 35:2–5; Hosea 2:13; Revelation 17:3–5; Isaiah 33:16–24; 1 Timothy 2:9–10; 1 Peter 3:3–5; 1 John 2:15–17.

The Bible records that a man came to Jesus one day asking: "Good Master, what good thing shall I do, that I may have eternal life?" Jesus' immediate response was, "if thou wilt enter into life, keep the commandments" (Matthew 19:16, 17). The answer Jesus gave surprises many today, for it is quite different than many assume He would have given. The standard answers, so popular today, are usually such things as repent, believe, be baptized, confess, etc.; but sadly, seldom does one hear "be obedient to God." When Jesus soon returns there will be many professed Christians who will be surprised to hear Him say, "depart from Me, ye that work iniquity" (Matthew 7:21- 23). Remember, iniquity is sin and "sin is the transgression of the law (1 John 3:4). Therefore, an appropriate paraphrase would be "Depart from Me, ye that reject and transgress My commandments." The relationship between love and obedience is clearly seen in such statements of Jesus as: "If you love me, keep my commandments" (John 14:15). "For this is the love of God, that we keep his commandments" (1 John 5:3). "Howbeit in vain do they worship me, teaching for doctrines the command-ments of men. For laying aside the commandment of God, ye hold the tradition of men" (Mark 7:7, 8). It is interesting that the only commandment God prefaced with the word "remember" is the very one the majority of the world has forgotten. When God brings this commandment to one's attention they are usually told by their reli-gious leaders not to concern themselves with it for it is now obsolete. This, however, should not come as a surprise for the word of God warned that there would be "false teachers" who would "bring in damnable heresies" and "many shall follow their pernicious ways" and the "truth shall be evil spoken of" (2 Peter 2:1-2). This has truly taken place today. Discover how in The Forgotten Commandment.

PO Box 136637
Fort Worth, TX 76163
(817)919-7267
www.fourthangelpublications.com

THE FOURTH ANGEL'S
PUBLISHING